AF334857

Cur aliquid vidi

ahsahta press

The New Series

number 8

Cur aliquid vidi

Lance Phillips

ahsahta press

Boise State University • Boise • Idaho • 2004

AHSAHTA PRESS, BOISE STATE UNIVERSITY
BOISE, IDAHO 83725
http://ahsahtapress.boisestate.edu

Copyright © 2004 by Lance Phillips

Printed in the United States of America.
Cover art: Marcel Duchamp, "The Illuminating Gas" from Etant Donnes. © 2004 Artists Rights
    Society (ARS), New York / ADAGP, Paris / Succession Marcel Duchamp.
First printing 2004.
ISBN 0-916272-82-6

Library of Congress Cataloging-in-Publication Data

Phillips, Lance, 1970-
Cur aliquid vidi / Lance Phillips.
    p. cm. -- (The new series ; no. 8)
ISBN 0-916272-82-6 (pbk. : alk. paper)
I. Title. II. Series: New series (Ahsahta Press) ; no. 8.

PS3616.H46C87 2004
811'.6--DC22

2004014346

Some of these texts first appeared in *Aufgabe, Chimera Review, Fence, The Gig, Gutcult, Interim,* and *Word for Word.*

To the memory of Roy G. Miller (5/19/1916–3/02/1999)

And always for Kelly, Caden and Landen

Contents

Seeing as

SUPPERADDING HANDCUP COLLARHAND UP SHAFT TO BEAD
TONGUE/RINGDOVE
I ENJOY SKIN TURNING IN BLUE-LUMP LATERAL AROUND
1] OHIO
2] THE UTOPIAN SOCIETY

SHE HIS CHEST THE LIFTING ONTO MOVING UP LEFT
A GRASSED-IN PLACE
THE WAY BITE IS AMMA
SPIRAL

INDEX THE DRAGGING UP UNDERSIDE FROM SAC

MIRRORING COMING INTO TRUNK GRIP

THE TEN AFFINITIES TO ORIFICE RED ABOVE
EITHER LATERAL

MIRRORING DRINKING GOURD

SAYING HIS MOVE
SURROUNDING ORIFICE ROSY OVAL
HOMOGENEOUS BONNET AND AIM
TOAD'S THE STRUCTURE AT SLEEP CONECIRCLECONE

HANDCUP THE EAST THE WEST

COLLARHAND THE NORTH THE SOUTH

AGAIN BOLT

FIG

THE FIGMILK CATALYZING PANSY EXTENDING EVERYWHERE

ROLLING OVER THE ONE THE OTHER FIG

WARMING LATERAL SURFACE WARMING-TO THUMB/NIPPLE

SPLIT FIG'S TWO ARCS ABUTMENT THEN ARROW FORCE
BETWEEN THE CHESTS BLUEWHITE

Cuneiformvalley

Splotch under arm the raising-to BACK
TO LAYING ON HER LEFT SIDE LAYING HER ON LEFT SIDE
BELLY

trying the the trying the pine leaves in winter

Collarwells the pocking up from wrists hypersensing the four
collar bones are fifteen

Hyperjunction the repetitions ORIFICE OVER TWO BOWLS
A DUST THE COLOR OF YOUR HAIR

Wasp jaw the cupping of use of place
HER GRIP RELEASE BEING THE CIRCUMFERENCE

Morning star/evening star mirroring the dragging the thumb nail over
Plan/blanc mirroring the dragging the thumb nail over

orifice BEGINNING WITH WILD GINGER

HYPERNOMOS
THE DRAWING UP AND OUT TO SLICK THE SKIN
DEERMOUSE

MOUTHHAIROVOID

BEAUTIFUL SOUL stringbean the coming from nerves
the number six into a snowcrust

METEMPSYCHOSIS THE ASSIMILATING STRUCTURE INTO
ABOVE HER CHEEKBONES

TIGHTEN

HAIRABUTMENTTRIANGLE
the raising a fine finch her back
CLAIMANT

form the 1800s leaving in houses to stay
THE TUGGING THE ONE ON RIGHT INTO MOUTH
SCALPGRIP   cities
The poppies
from the 1800s living in houses to stay the people

Now this (word) "he ascended," what is it

TAKING DOWN-OVER NOSE CHIN HER KNUCKLE MAKING THE
CHAIN THE NOISE MUTUAL AUTHORITY

a-tapping the tree

THE INCH FROM KNUCKLE DRAGGING TO THE RIGHT HER
SPINE DOWN TO BUTTOCK UP THEN THE LEFT TO NECK

THIS watertreestag to accomplish a place

CHARACTERIZATION

FRAME

fine wing willowshred grievous

PACING

CONTROLLED VOCABULARY
A

CONTEMPLATIVE SOUL THIS it was is Venus
thumb peaking to knuckle tugging orifice
down West that way

TONETENORGRAFT lay as a triangle up from the bed

making entering be fistfullwithhair over each shoulder
CONTEMPLATIVESOULVERUMFACTUM "if I didn't touch him"

the chrysanthemum
having been the former present folds same with her lips

VERUMFACTUM had I not touched him

WHAT DIFFERENCE IS THERE AND REPEAT A LITTLE

bite tightening the skin to definition to nipple
at hearing the shapes TRIANGLE CIRCLE   SPIRAL

centipede a covering then brownred

centipede uncovering PSEUDOS close to the ground
Hermes being chair, northmost chair

MONASTIC CYCLOPEAN MONARCHIC

   the R's fractal surface iterating scar above tendon's slope to ankle
being made bulge, excitation

CRACK

The rounding into throat

Writing the WHAT DIFFERENCE IS THERE over the WHAT IS DIFFERENCE
As moon

the PSEUDOS lamb to BY WATCHING
THE TUGGING ONE THE OTHER INTO MOUTH SMOOTHING THE SKIN
a flint flit sparrows EVERYBODY KNOWS

From EYEHOLE/HECATE breadth of kelp

Upwards of VALUATION knuckle drawn from lash

sporing in as much coherence from his stick
along side sense a tree a cloud

sporing in as much self-analysis from his stick
along side sense the "like grapes"

BETISTAPARA-SENSETREACHERY

the crooking toward his thumb over his stick
normal   Scylla

The "midst of" equaling both designation and barking

Indicating along side sense the splitting his lip

PORCELAINERRORSUN

Habitus

Adjunct field

Captivated   Seed Apollonian Aresian Athenian the squirrel
pokes into   When artery out from her neck divides the lower
quadrant to each breast

Soul   Red a hollow back from lips jawbone ear
So distinctly a sound "decentrist" "poppy" his "where's it come
from"

Biting above her collarbone taking the materiality
the rhododendron leaves taking reliant

Realliance the icicles

Clear idea the real ideas Leech Higher Man folded into
mouth-to-brain   Transactioning his hand presses eye over cheekbone
for whose tree's
the anything

    Gets

    Intention only the one color red-orange

    Goodsense   The folding into mouth the brain
Mercurial the ant and grass

    Gets

The marking off about paradoxy
6 (i.e. a perfect number) black and white freshwater clams

Horse demultiplying into the shadow of our holding his backpack
commonsense

Architectonic

The thumb fattening into wrist for effect

Two windows giving shape definition the tree
appears apple and pear lighted

Conversatio

Field-gradient-threshold

ComposingSoul
re-implicating here participle   the boat left burning before the
creek   ass and lion wolf and sheep in the body to have butterfly
be grip   focusing the thumbs into Metaschematism

The little statements

Pear wood bowl   Helen non-representing tree
each the four principles of reason

Ratio cognoscendi   Ratio fiendi   Ratio essendi   Ratio agendi
The little phhhf
stem wells into her palm

Using the apostate tyrant as his tool

Metexein   The dough-skin   Red smoke
placing along side leg stiffening into curveback the silver hairs

Contain

Inverts from beaked head the chair the re-championing windows
resplendent

Only willow sticks

1226   Learns nature
skink roseroot corresponding to basket   Object   Purely head
loving her condition

Only willow sticks

Franciseurydiceownership

Theft   The touching his touch undershirt and rice
especially resonance the took

Intensity-linkage-resonance-forced

Excending deer rosebush
the talking about red color and the seeing red color

Think you should put it in there

Of

Third estate   Property properly the deer and rosebush
uhrrr

Thick should   No polis up entwining esophagus
but passing between shadow the cookie

A-feeling a-thinking fabric

Apparition   1226   The object surface cusp
cut/cup   They combine selfish appearance
and the sugar

The age gods heroes   The age people

Of

Well ass or wolf and sheep   Of in

Invention   Societal   Very clear the wires repartitioning Confused Concept in crocus nearly touching the wall

Well invented society   "Everything is one to the extent that every thing is different"

Paunch   Hegemony   Black
Re-championing specific difference crow the sugar

Arch-empiricist
The correspondence invisible in arbor his house
and what's pink thing

This

Biformity   Flat-eye

Down to adrenal glands the snow the mind it won't make it move
his feeling of blue leg   Innovation

The right   Cup thigh lift push

Orpheusownership

Rub
Microordering adrenal glands to windpipe to armpits
Space to people-king   Sovereign yellow skin

Moisteye

Turn me on side

Forming the full his leg   blankets
once pressed

I am baffled   The act chair near touching

Gnomologium

Five hotter smaller nights
Cuffs passing through lip producing "he's dying"
five halters night
smaller halters night

Saying it effectively "chariot" touching near bed

Something (a liquid)

The clutch pear blossoms of it

Proud converting off his skin
reap rapping into the brass frame

Lif-ting lif-ting

He winked efforts

    Props up his body good chair calling the name for it paradise
black good birds rise

There are two Times
he is having been his body and due to it will

Leftfoot

Takes pity   The fffff
box

Some triangles with the bruises encircling them   Definite light

Balsam   Began speaking he gave them him   Real white

The people this paradox

Are
The dying of in bird

Whose is trust   Of course the twinkling beginning oily grass
perpendicular to fox

The rest compose that man back seat

—metastabilizing the two trees / not truth but convenience
—a head with smile a theta
—ISN'T

"It talks to me mostly it hums"   Anger
sure at the concern with position
in mind and extending into topos   The deepest is the skin

Holding in hyacinth
wild system

—Division vs. analysis

If it is day it is a scratch in two parts east
her spine

Of
Day it is red

Eyelimb   Reclamation the acting of   Feathers mark the eye
at top   Head/Hecate

—the beginning "did it"   Many
—his lips purple-brown the gods heroes monsters
—reason a full body blanketing the body
—color full body blanketing in reflect absorb

Nihil motum ex antiquo probabile est

Passions-bodies   The ideas reversible to egg
their ethics

Sure anger   Were nymphs will be trees
being identitarian

His "each tree they are similar with my hand"

Smaller

Sectioning sky expressed as sparrow

Four thousand per hour up to self

Boatman

greenflash in bringing it to mouth the sun from a book
—IS
—BRUJO   HAIR LIGHTENING A CLOUD JUST ABOVE

The pre-fixing with alpha—there is no time without people when it
Isn't protecting—begins objectifying barking and dog

RED TWO

Wind splitting lily rows
Lilies of
If it is day and orange   Policy
Purely affirmation
Her pulling apart up

Puckering up from the bed

—conexa
    Sets

—conjuncta
    Its my gift pillbug

—disjuncta
    Attributes tree
    44,000   Today with nothing
    Grasses   Dollars   Trains

Scallion salt coriander

You're that hierarchy
You're creating that hierarchy

Chup   The leaves of trees

Coming up from tugs out lip
Head with kisses

Prouder silver underwing it has

layering   Aion

Puckering lips forward then left off to the door
as telling
Good object   Massive-meager   Bluebird
suggestive the "the ghosts skinny persons windows"

Of   Fly

Spark corn meal jeweled day and night

like and foot = pedestal
like and blood = crimson
Helios   Splinter bisectioning his toe into theta

—quasi-cause stylus flycatcher
—you smell the same the bathwater
as
   Warming isolating arm

   HAS

   To green   neither the tree nor the color
is   Bath/Diana/an auto-eroticism: this-side

   This very sweet spot

—his ball hitting the blackbird is a flesh

TUCK

   Rolling over orifice fig
abdomen

   Full well sun getting Glistens at "it gets"

   Line and point horsetails
   Running from collar well some water roots "parable" in disjunction

clear

It is very easy—Each seed from its mouth—Counter-tyrant

DIGS

Pinch—Monstorum—Softsac

Monday/Sunday

Perversion—a pear leaf into Troy—the subverse—leafgreen from
nipple to throat
    Parrhesia

    Sweet william viola is it

Structuring everything in the room both hair and skin
into mouth

Orpheusneck the stem of sweet pea

Ease the rubbing foot up over the other back of analysis

good person

De nobis fabula narratur

                    corporealizing Adriadne
          corporealizing of middle thigh I feel   Apples

          A very sturdy sun

          —squeezing it in hands
          —mistakenly the laurel as two persons

          SLIP

Personal purity

Ah   How flaring out from the dragging over orifice
returning radish & honey for them

Red from jaw to chest

—it is very easy "The branch clouds"

Cardinal out from conflating into three fingers

Yes going to say a stair skink
going towards neither mind nor reason nor thought nor
consciousness nor soul nor will nor truth

Clear crease down along arm/Hektor/Inked eaten rose

Clasping behind the head hand/atropos

OCCUPANCY

—arms his occupancies are

on the coriander white
hegemony with that book Sun

            in testicles
            in ovaries
            in brain
yellow ending lily

Oh yes the touching quite a lot/ Having miraculating the surface be
window/ table

Chrysanthemum or any rose

Is what is use is by
breast his mouth produced/ work surface into each leg from the table
shinning-walled

Symbolic vs. imaginary

There's a great grey box today
between mons pubis and buttocks

the sky
of course true spermatozoa

HERALDRY/ORIFICE

Lack

Bird/ Flutter in the bowel/ Vestal conscripting
hearth flame/ lay

Love work and knowledge the mouth the anus the aural openings
yielding day lilies

Hill skull this

Either or or the place

Two mounds abdominal flesh they took for breasts

Sperm sheening hand back   Basil and mint for them

Lion ass ceiling sun for them
cohering in as much room as possible

Thumb the four fingers producing what is the tree from his forehead

leaf
I am sorry

on mudwasp out from orifice mnemotechnics

The two incisors sprung from tree
horn attached to his body drawing up teeth

From her hand to her mouth point at which there's a bird

HAMMER

forked branch   The belly warming down on orifice from a book the
apples bruising an exit
for themselves

EYE-HAND-VOICE/ geographism
Taste this sack ringed as it pleases let me

Functionaries the voiding sunflower turn   Box/ Clock

So many

Voice

    —sun

Graphism

    —germinal between belly & groin what does close to the sun

About the Author

Lance Phillips is author of *Corpus Socius* (Ahsahta Press, 2002). He lives in Charlotte, North Carolina, with his wife, son, and daughter. He writes and manages the weblogs Coursing Public Thought (http://www.lancephillips.blogspot.com) and Here Comes Everybody (http://herecomeseverybody.blogspot.com).

Ahsahta Press

SAWTOOTH POETRY PRIZE SERIES

2002: AARON McCOLLOUGH, *Welkin* (Brenda Hillman, judge)
2003: GRAHAM FOUST, *Leave the Room to Itself* (Joe Wenderoth, judge)
2004: NOAH ELI GORDON, *The Area of Sound Called the Subtone* (Claudia Rankine, judge)

NEW SERIES

DAN BEACHY-QUICK, *Spell*
LISA FISHMAN, *Dear, Read*
PEGGY HAMILTON, *Forbidden City*
CHARLES O. HARTMAN, *Island*
LANCE PHILLIPS, *Corpus Socius*
LANCE PHILLIPS, *Cur aliquid vidi*
HEATHER SELLERS, *Drinking Girls and Their Dresses*
LIZ WALDNER, *Saving the Appearances*

MODERN AND CONTEMPORARY POETRY OF THE AMERICAN WEST

SANDRA ALCOSSER, *A Fish to Feed All Hunger*
DAVID AXELROD, *Jerusalem of Grass*
DAVID BAKER, *Laws of the Land*
DICK BARNES, *Few and Far Between*
CONGER BEASLEY, JR., *Over DeSoto's Bones*
LINDA BIERDS, *Flights of the Harvest-Mare*
RICHARD BLESSING, *Winter Constellations*
BOYER, BURMASTER, AND TRUSKY, EDS., *The Ahsahta Anthology*
PEGGY POND CHURCH, *New and Selected Poems*

This book is set in Apollo type with ITC Oficina Serif titles
by Ahsahta Press at Boise State University
and manufactured on acid-free paper
by Boise State University Printing and Graphics, Boise, Idaho.

AHSAHTA PRESS

2004

JANET HOLMES, DIRECTOR